Filling Your *Emptiness*

Your New Life

James Ivey, MSM and Claudia Ivey

Collaboration by Claudia Ivey

ISBN 979-8-88644-814-6 (Paperback)
ISBN 979-8-88644-815-3 (Digital)

Covenant Books
11661 Hwy 707
Murrells Inlet, SC 29576
www.covenantbooks.com

To Claudia

Most important of all, this effort is dedicated to my Christ-loving, caring, patient, continually forgiving wife, Claudia. Claudia was the person who I saw when I finally hit the lowest moment of my life's despair and looked up. She, for whatever reason, was attracted to this wayward, desolate, suicidal, beyond-hope, vagabond party animal. She was the beginning glimmer of hope that grew in spite of my reluctance and resistance. She persevered through the many bumpy roads, detours, and dead-ends. She is the influence that resulted in the salvation of all three of our sons—the most fitting example of Jesus's loving perseverance and grace.

To Kate Ivey, Licensed Professional Counselor, MA, LPC, PMH-C

Counseling is a place to safely and gently lean into any struggles, pain points, fears, hopes, and goals alongside a trained professional who bears witness with nonjudgmental acceptance and full confidentiality. It is a place where dignity is affirmed and shame is broken down, so that healing and freedom can be experienced. Counseling can involve feedback from the therapist that may look like offering observations, considering various perspectives, education, strategy and skill building, and encouragement.

(https://www.iveycounselingcenter.com/)

Kate is the inspiration behind this written effort.

Contents

Foreword

Kate Ivey, MA, LPC, PMH-C, licensed professional counselor

I have the unique perspective of being a trauma therapist and also being James's daughter-in-law. I must admit I knew very little about the severity of his childhood trauma until recently. Bits and pieces of his childhood have come out in stories at family dinners, and I once watched a video of him giving his testimony where he shared some details, but only after reading James's book did the full gravity of his trauma leave me simultaneously in awe of his resilience and breathless from what he had to endure. In this book he gives a detailed description of what generational trauma looks like, and he shares his life-and-death battle to break free.

James describes a childhood that is infiltrated with complex trauma. Trauma is described as exposure to an event in which a person fears for their life or the life of another, believes they will be injured, or their bodily integrity will suffer (National Childhood Traumatic Stress Network). The result of this exposure is both an emotional and physical stress response that lasts even after the event has passed. Complex trauma occurs when exposures are repeated and pervasive. All trauma can impact brain, physical, emotional, relational, and spiritual development. However, complex trauma, especially in childhood, often reveals the worst outcomes for a person as they grow older. Without enough protective factors, a person who has experienced childhood and/or complex trauma suffers from exponentially more health problems, addictive and high-risk behaviors, attachment disruptions, and suicidal thoughts (among many other problems). If a person with childhood trauma grows up and suffers from these issues in adulthood and they marry and have children, they are almost destined to repeat the cycle. Almost.

Yet James's story is one of *hope, healing,* and *cycle breaking*!

To put cycle breaking simply, a person needs to have enough resiliency factors to make a change. Some resiliency factors are internal (personality, work ethic, talents, strengths), and many are external (people, mentors, financial stability, community safety, opportunity, and access). As I read his story from a trauma-informed lens, James's persistent search for security and love ultimately leads him to finally recognize it when he meets Claudia, his wife. She is what we call a resiliency factor—someone that could see in James what he couldn't see in himself. When James ultimately finds his true identity in Jesus's abundant and steadfast love, he could finally know he wouldn't be left alone in his pain or his healing.

In this book, James makes the case that Jesus was his ultimate resiliency factor. Through Jesus's love that was made known to James first by Claudia, he was able to recognize Jesus's orchestration of healing through people, opportunities, and a good old-fashioned growing desire in James for goodness. A desire for something better for his marriage, his children, his grandchildren—and a belief that he could actually change the generational cycles. That is where I come in! I have been on the receiving end of James's healing and witnessed firsthand how Jesus's love has resulted in a family legacy that is no longer bound by trauma. James and Claudia have sons that are incredibly wonderful husbands and fathers. They have grandchildren that know abundant love, safety, security, and hope. And when I consider what James endured as a child, I cannot help but get the chills at the reality of this verse:

> Glory to God, who is able to do far beyond all that we could ask or imagine by his power at work within us; glory to him in the church and in Christ Jesus for all generations, forever and always. Amen! (Ephesians 3:20–21)

Mary Brewer, director, New Beginnings Recovery Center

Though Jim Ivey has had a life full of hurt and trauma, he has turned his pain into gain. He is using the events from an abusive and overwhelming childhood to help heal others from their pain.

God has used Jim's story to bring life to the hurting and downtrodden. He has a powerful message of hope and healing that anyone and everyone should know about. Whether you have had an abusive childhood or not, his story will help someone that you know.

Every American is affected by addiction. Jim has walked the walk and is now giving practical solutions to the hurting heart.

If you have a family member that is suffering from addiction, they need to read this book.

It is an honor to know Jim, and I encourage everyone to take to heart the practical solutions in this book.

Email: mary@nbr-services.com

Phone: (720) 473-7106, (303) 830-2064

Fred Bapp, counselor, Breaking the Cycle of Addiction

In my view, the recovery-relapse cycle may be broken by acknowledging three realities:

1. I am running away from my problems and alcohol, drugs, or other addictive behaviors and providing a powerful hiding place from my pain while bringing about eventually a living death.
2. I am searching for meaning in my life.
3. I am attempting to connect with others socially to find acceptance—maybe even caring.

In all of the above, the recovering addict needs to find ways of dealing with triggers of relapse by embracing the need for relief and connection by communicating: I know I want to drink/use, but I will not give the thought what it is saying it wants. Instead, I will ask my addictive self, "What can I give you?" rather than relapsing.

Beautiful examples may be found in spiritual searches, alone or powerfully with others. AA and Celebrate Recovery come to mind quickly.

A higher power, for those of us who invite Jesus Christ into our lives, becomes a loved-filled reality. We no longer have to be held captive by the need to mood-alter. We have embraced our total selves through him, Jesus. We have an indwelling relationship available 24-7!

Praise me, praise you, praise God!

*****

Professional commentary was provided by Kate Ivey, licensed professional counselor, MA, LPC, PMH-C; Mary Brewer, director, New Beginnings Recovery Center; and Fred Bapp, licensed counselor.

Mary Brewer, director

New Beginnings Recovery Center (NBRC)
An Addiction Treatment Model That Builds Foundations in Bedrock™
16 Years: Helping Thousands Stay Clean and Sober
A Comprehensive Recovery Program Healing Addiction
Improving Mental Health

A high honor for our treatment programs and services, NBRC has earned the Joint Commission's Gold Seal of Approval accreditation/certification.

Everything we do in our treatment program is dedicated to giving our clients a new life by healing the mind, body, and spirit. We deliver a total quality care addiction treatment program utilizing an evidence-based curriculum, guiding our clients through every step in the recovery process. By providing a fully integrated addiction treatment regime, *you can break the cycle of addiction and change your behavior.*

NBRC services:

Residential Inpatient and Outpatient Recovery
Supplemental Care and Services
Clean & Sober Living Care Programs
Substance Use Disorder
Co-Occurring Mental Illness

Opioid Treatment
Drug Treatment
Alcohol Treatment

We continually review, modify, and deploy state-of-the-science therapies to better support our clients.

www.newbeginningsrecoverydenver.com

Email: mary@nbr-services.com

Frederick Byron Bapp, licensed counselor

Fred attended Baylor University, where he graduated with a degree in social work. Fred received his master's in social work from Florida State University and was a social worker for over fifty years, including three decades at Colorado West in the mountains of Eagle, Colorado.

Fred began working at New Beginnings Recovery Center, Littleton, Colorado, in 2014 as a group therapist. Fred continued to love counseling, sharing his faith and making new friends even up to his death. Fred was an avid marathon runner, completing over fifty full marathons in many US states.

Most important to Fred was his faith in Jesus Christ, with many of his writings reflecting his faith. He was deeply religious and an avid churchgoer. Fred was known for his puns and poetry. He has published three books, with the latest, *Addictions, Love and Recovery.*

I will greatly miss Fred. He will also be missed by countless coworkers, friends, and patients.

Introduction

Filling Your Emptiness

Regardless of your current life situation, everyone has an "emptiness" that creates doubt, disappointment, sadness, loneliness, pain. The "emptiness" continually surfaces, causing personal questioning, self-doubt, confusion that can cause discouragement, conflict, turmoil, anger, aggression, oppression, depression, rejection, self-harm.

It matters not your age, race, physique, education, finance, or social affluence—popular or neglected, everyone is continually haunted by their "emptiness."

The people around us and our environment influence our reaction to our emptiness. We seek to fill our emptiness. We try anything and everything that we are exposed to in an attempt to achieve happiness, success, fulfillment.

We seek to fill our emptiness by overworking, overexercising, over-entertaining, overeating, social media addiction, shopping addiction, gambling addiction, alcohol, drugs, opioids, pornography. None provide the long-lasting happiness, self-worth, or fulfillment we seek. Many of our repeated practices become habits, addictions, cycles.

There is only one answer and choice to truly, continually, and successfully filling your emptiness with what provides the life of acceptance and everlasting love you seek.

God says,

> You know that in the past the way you were living was useless. It was a way of life you learned from those who lived before you. (1 Peter 1:18 ERV)
>
> This way of life was handed down to you by your own people, but, I set you free from this empty way of life. (1 Peter 1:18 NIRV)
>
> I have loved you with a love that lasts forever. I have continued loving you with a kindness that never fails. (Jeremiah 31:3)

God's will and plan for your new life:

> Jesus said, "I came that you may have life and have it abundantly. My purpose is to give you a rich and satisfying life." (John 10:10)

What is a cycle?

- Any complete series of occurrences that repeats or is repeated.
- A sequence of changing states that, upon completion, produces a final state identical to the original one.

What is a tradition?

- A long-established or inherited way of thinking or acting.
- The handing down of statements, beliefs, legends, customs, information, etc. from generation to generation, especially by word of mouth or by practice.

Tradition implies voluntary participation, choice. One can choose whether or not to continue. One is not bound or destined to accept, practice, or continue such.

Out of tradition, many people will not walk under a ladder, fearing bad luck.

Many people practice a tradition of washing their hands before meals for hygiene purposes.

Many people say a blessing of thanks before their meals.

Many people believe wearing shoes in one's house is courteous, while many countries feel it is rude.

Many Christians participate in Halloween, while many Christians do not.

Traditions, over changing times, economies, and cultures, can become very confusing. They may even become stumbling blocks or breaking points of ideology and friendships: interracial marriage, interfaith marriage, common law marriage, etc.

But the key to traditions is their voluntary nature.

Cycles, on the other hand, are a reoccurring event regardless of one's belief or willingness of acceptance or personal choice.

A successful plant life cycle is the same in any part of our world, and it does not vary due to changing circumstances. There are five stages of the plant life cycle: seed germination, growth, reproduction, pollination, and seed-spreading stages.

A year is traditionally comprised of spring, summer, autumn, and winter. The attributes of each season can vary greatly between Alaska, Colorado, and Florida, but the seasons are a regular cycle event.

A winter in Alaska and Florida could not be more different. Yet a winter in Colorado, overall, is greatly different from either of those two at times, yet possibly similar at other times.

Some people believe there are also inescapable human addictions, including kleptomania, workaholism, alcoholism, drug addiction, abuse (domestic, child, sexual), etc. It is widely believed, even clinically, that an alcoholic's children will be prone to alcoholism, that a child abuse victim will become a child abuser, etc.

What is an addiction?

Practice: the action or process of performing or doing something.

Habit: an acquired behavior pattern regularly followed until it has become almost involuntary.

Vice: immoral conduct; depraved or degrading behavior.

Addiction: craving, dependence, obsession, enslavement; state of being compulsively committed to a habit or practice or to something that is psychologically or physically habit-forming, such as narcotics, to such an extent that its cessation causes severe trauma.

Types of addiction:

- Food addiction
- Sex addiction
- Internet addiction
- Pornography addiction
- Technology addiction (computers, laptops, tablets, pads, cell phones, etc.)
- Social media addiction
- Video game addiction
- Work addiction
- Exercise addiction
- Spiritual obsession (not to be confused with religious devotion)
- Seeking pain
- Cutting
- Shopping addiction
- Gambling addiction
- Drug addiction: alcohol, tobacco, opioids, prescription drugs (sedatives, hypnotics, or anxiolytics like sleeping pills and tranquilizers), cocaine, cannabis, amphetamines, hallucinogens, inhalants, phencyclidine (PCP, etc.).

List of impulsive disorders (where impulses cannot be resisted, which could be considered a type of addiction):

- Intermittent explosive disorder (compulsive aggressive and assault acts)
- Kleptomania (compulsive stealing)

- Pyromania (compulsive setting of fires)

There are many similarities between substance addiction and behavioral addiction. Some of the similarities include the excitement or "high" resulting from use or behavior, craving the high, development of tolerance leading to increased use or repeated behavior, loss of control, and psychological and physical withdrawal symptoms.

Signs of addiction

Addiction manifests itself differently in each person, and signs of addiction vary based on what the person is addicted to. Drug addiction changes the body, specifically the brain, and can have visible physical side effects. Behavioral addiction does not exhibit the same physical symptoms that accompany drug and alcohol addiction or substance abuse.

Dependency is when a person needs something in order to function normally and is often accompanied by increased tolerance and symptoms of withdrawal when the drug or behavior is no longer present. It is a gateway to addiction. A person can be dependent without being addicted if it does not cause a person to engage in compulsive or harmful behavior. If you find yourself or a loved one becoming dependent on any substance or behavior, it is important to seek help as soon as possible to avoid getting to the point of addiction, which is even more difficult to overcome.

Addiction, whether physical or behavioral, impacts many parts of a person's life. Repeated use of substances or repeated behaviors results in physical brain changes, leading to impaired learning, decision-making, memory, and judgment. Over time, addiction causes organ damage and increases risk of contracting a communicable disease. Addiction is known to cause depression and/or suicide and affects relationships with family and friends. Legal problems and financial woes are also common issues that result from addiction.

Thus, traditions are voluntary. Cycles can be repetitive and seemingly involuntary. Addictions can become physiological.

In reality, some human conditions (bipolar, alcoholism, etc.) can be physiologically prompted, but can be treated. Other conditions, such as abuse, is voluntary, but may need assistance to "break its cycle" of reoccurrence.

"Cycling" from one generation to the next is not predestined and *can* be broken/treated successfully. This information will be discussed in detail with examples, symptoms, practices, treatments, and sources for "breaking the cycle" and creating your new life.

Just because my father's violent alcoholism was seemingly passed from his father and may have been physiologically "triggered" and could most certainly have a case for psychological cause, his abuse was voluntary. I, with great care and assistance, did not become a violent alcoholic or physical abuser.

People of My Cycle

Dysfunction: cycles of repeated failure.

Father

My father was a violent abusive alcoholic. He had at least two failed divorced marriages. He provided no support for my family. Becoming a public embarrassment and nuisance, he was sentenced in and out of numerous state hospitals for treatment of his alcoholism.

My childhood memories are of being awakened in the middle of nights by him violently beating my mother. I would sit up in my bed crying as my older brothers hid their heads under their pillows. I would beat my tiny fists into my pillow, wishing I could do something.

During one night's beating, I actually yelled aloud, "Stop it!" He quickly came into our bedroom yelling and held a pistol to my head, shouting, "You want some of this?" Tears poured down my face. I was in a catatonic state and could not speak.

I lived in continual fear. I swore I'd never be like him! I swore I'd never drink!

I can never in my life remember him telling me "I love you."

Mother

My mother had numerous failed divorced marriages. She left and divorced her first husband during his military boot camp and returned home pregnant with my half sister. My mother would have me and my two older brothers with my father.

My mother would provide the full family support because of my father's drunkenness. She was always at work, busy, or tired. She often blamed us children for not helping to "stop my father's beatings." We were often alone, neglected, and "nothing but trouble."

Paternal grandfather

My paternal grandfather, who died before my birth, I was told, was an alcoholic/drunk.

My grandfather, Earnest E. Kellum, whose mother died during his birth, and older brother Bob and sister Sarah/Ella were given to a Houston, Texas, orphanage. Earnest was adopted by a local farming family named Ivey. Bob and Ella were never adopted, but did visit Earnest as he grew up. Bob never married. Ella did and is now deceased. No more information is known about Ella or her family. I know nothing regarding my original Kellum family roots.

Paternal grandmother

My paternal grandmother, Viola, had numerous failed marriages/divorces.

Rumor has it she wouldn't pay for Ernest's grave/funeral because he was a drunk. She was always partial to my Uncle James, the oldest of her three sons, because my father, Thomas, and Uncle Ray were both drunks.

My father's son from his first failed marriage, Rodney, was bedridden and speechless his entire twenty-one years and required constant care, which my father did not provide. My grandmother gave Rodney away for care to my Uncle James. She paid for a new house for them in a far distant part of the state as well. She would also later give away my other uncle's two adopted Hispanic children.

Maternal grandmother

My maternal grandmother, Mae, had numerous failed marriage/divorces. She constantly criticized my mother. She was always partial to my half sister and openly detested my brothers and me.

Half sister

My half sister had numerous failed marriages and partners. Her first husband was with another woman while she delivered their only son in a military hospital.

We once allowed her and one partner to live with us "between rental moves" with broken promises of house care and the price of a rental moving truck due to her own "unexpected" rejected credit card.

Oldest brother

My oldest brother was the first to start college (with my mother's help and loans). He flunked out the first year for partying too much. At his next college, he lived in a "party house" with four to six others and partied endlessly. Through this influence, I began my use of alcohol and drugs. I can still remember the very first drink I ever took as he handed a bottle of Bacardi Rum over into the back seat to me. I sat there momentarily, hesitating and remembering my promise to never drink, but the fun and companionship was too much to resist.

Upon his eventual graduation, I secured grocery store jobs for him and several friends to move to Denver. They did not come, nor did he call to explain, leaving me quite embarrassed. The next time he called for jobs for five people, I refused to help until they actually arrived, though I did loan him a small amount of money for the move (which he took six years repaying). Without notice, three arrived.

A number of years later, he walked out on his wife and two small children to live with another woman. He later divorced and ceased all communication—at least with us.

I helped his former wife and children until I became aware they were both working together to use me and take advantage of my generosity.

To my knowledge, he has never met his two grandsons, Troy and Ryan. He has never met any of my nine grandchildren or two of my sons.

Next older brother

My next older brother had numerous failed marriages/divorces and live-in mates. He did not finish high school. As a mechanic, he quit working when his auto repair shop was robbed late one night and all his tools were stolen. He filed for worker's compensation for "supposed back injuries" but was rejected. He lived at home for free to care for my mother, supposedly, per my half sister, taking her money when desired.

As you can see from these examples of *all* the people of influence in my family, the many repeated failed lives over generations seemed to demonstrate reoccurring cycles.

Circumstances of My Cycle

The circumstances of your life do not define you. How you react to your circumstances does define you!

Murder next door

Please remember that I was the youngest child in this dysfunctional family. So in most occurrences, though understanding may have been vague, memory was not. At the time, few things had relevance or made sense to me, nor in most cases did they really matter.

This changed as I grew older, and some things did not "register" until my adulthood. There were times as I learned or experienced life that I may have had an epiphany and thought, *Wow, now I get it!*

One such occurrence was when we moved from our very old and small house on "busy" Ninth Street to Seventh Street and Twitchell Avenue.

In the Ninth Street house, I shared a bedroom with two brothers and my half sister. Ninth Street was one of the main traffic arteries and always seemed to have lots of traffic on its two lanes. The Seventh Street house thus had more rooms, and there was less traffic. Though at one time when my sister was in high school and dating,

Seventh Street seemed to be an integral part of the "dragging main" route on Friday and Saturday nights. I'm not sure if the route was tradition or because of my sister.

But the house itself was the epiphany. In moving in, it had a curiosity to me that all the windows were nailed shut from the inside of the rooms. The windows in the rooms on the east house side all had heavy blinds and curtains. All three doors to the house had at least two locks and screen doors with at least two lock latches. I would soon find out why!

In 1943, there had been two murders in the home directly next door to the east. A Dr. Roy Hunt and his wife, Mae Frank, had been murdered in a late-night seemingly arranged "paid killing for hire." (See this article: https://texoso66.com/2019/08/29/dr-and-mrs-roy-hunt-murders-unsolved-mystery/.)

My dysfunctional family had bought the house next door! A house no one else wanted anything to do with, except my poor family, who savored a cheap buy to safety or peace of mind. I would spend many a night being laughed at and traumatized, going to bed with the covers over my head.

Littlefield, Texas (KCBD): October 26, 1943, is a day that left the community of Littlefield in shock.

Dana Samuelson writes about the day Dr. Roy Hunt and his wife, Mae Frank, were found murdered in their home and the investigation that followed. Her book *Clovis Road* details a rumored love triangle between Dr. Hunt and Ruth Newton, the wife of his med school classmate.

The author says Dr. Newton hired someone to kill the couple. He appeared in trial numerous times to appeal the case.

The niece of Dr. Hunt tells us the community went from leaving their doors unlocked to being too scared to go outside.

(https://texoso66.com/2019/08/29/dr-and-mrs-roy-hunt-murders-unsolved-mystery/
https://www.lubbockonline.com/story/lifestyle/columns/2017/12/01/chronicles-tangled-web-west-texas-murders/14825468007/
https://casetext.com/case/thomas-v-state-232)

That scar on my neck!

I have a haunting memory as a very young child—I believe around four years of age. Many people say a person can't remember things at that age, except possibly because of trauma. My memory is extremely traumatic.

I remember being carried into the local hospital screaming in dire pain. My vision and sight were blurred by the tears pouring out of my face, but I vividly remember being rushed into the hospital, turning right, rushing past the wall of thick square glass bricks, then left, down a seemingly long corridor.

I was to be treated for an extreme burn to the right side of my face. This burn would require a skin graft from my thigh.

The burn was the result of the explosion of a glass vaporizer that had overheated once its full content of water had been vaporized. When there was no longer any water for the heating element to vaporize out over the round metal cylinder used to house medicated salve, the element and glass jar exploded, expelling all pieces throughout the room. The metal container hit me in the right cheek below the eye, resulting in the extreme burn but, luckily, not losing my eye.

All of this was the result of having a childhood cold and being "put to bed," forgotten, neglected, and "nothing but trouble."

Musician, not!

As a young child, I once performed (sang?) a song on a local CBS TV affiliate Channel 13 program in Lubbock, Texas, called Jack Huddle's Children's Theater.

Jack Huddle was a West Texas rockabilly musician and song-writer. He performed and recorded with Buddy Holly early in Holly's career (Wikipedia).

At a very young age, I was very neatly dressed and taken to Lubbock early one morning. We arrived at some unknown location and were ushered into a building with many people scurrying around.

Being separated from my mother, I was taken into a "studio" and seated with many other young children in a peanut gallery sitting location. Someone read a list of instructions that were not heard as my giant eyes surveyed the premises.

At one point, a tall giant of a cowboy, armed with a guitar, came on the stage. He talked a lot and then sang some songs.

Suddenly, the captives of our peanut gallery were taken, one by one, out to stage center to talk with this giant cowboy. Then suddenly, he began playing his guitar, and the child began singing.

In great anxiety, I remember watching and fearing what was in evidence about to happen to me! But then as each child finished their musical humiliation, they were led to a side stage location and allowed to pick a packaged surprise gift.

With less trepidation, when my time came, I marched straight to center stage with eyes glued to the side stage packaged prize board. I answered, without realization, some questions asked by Cowboy Bob.

Then suddenly, he asked, "What song will you be singing for us today?" I froze! How could I be so ill prepared and freely sacrificed for such humiliation!

Something or someone prompted me back to reality (I'm sure Cowboy Bob had a prepared methodology for this type occurrence). "Sing?" I had to sing a Western song…*now*…on TV…in front of the whole world (a small child has no understanding of what a TV world is)!

Prompted back to reality, I searched my mind for a song. Nothing materialized. Blankly, I stared at Bob and noticed his eyebrows begin to slowly dip. Alas, I began singing "Home on the Range," the same song that had just been sung by the previous singer.

The only memory afterward was clutching my prize package!

Don't go to Grandma's house!

My aunt, who was my mother's younger sister, and uncle were not able to have their own children. So they arranged and secured two separate children, a girl, then a boy. These children were from Hispanic families that could not care for these unplanned newborns.

My aunt and uncle loved and cared for these children. As a cousin, I was never aware they were not my natural relatives or that they were Hispanic.

Unfortunately, my paternal grandmother hated these children with a passion. Though it seemed she hated everything pretty much equally.

On one occasion, my aunt and uncle—I am assuming by agreement—delivered the two small children to her for an afternoon of babysitting care. This would allow them time to go shopping at the closest big town.

Upon returning from their shopping trip, they were not allowed to enter the house, and there were no children to retrieve. While my aunt and uncle had spent the afternoon away shopping, my grandmother gave the children away. She had called a family to come and take the children. She paid this couple enough money to leave the state and have no further communication with anyone in our area.

My aunt and uncle were not allowed in the house because, as expected, they were mad enough and wanted to kill my grandmother.

So any time my siblings and I heard we were going to Grandma's house, we trembled with fear. We were not sure if any of us would be coming back!

Racism—there is no winner in this race

As a young child, I remember visits to the town's small library. It was located in the basement of the county courthouse.

As you entered the courthouse, you would take the stairs to the basement floor. At the bottom of the stairs, you would choose to turn left or right. To the right, about three doors down was the library. To the left were restrooms and then county government offices.

This was in the early 1950s. This is a lasting memory for me as it was symbolic of those days.

The restrooms were labeled boldly for both men and women. There were *two* for each: "Men: White Only," "Men: Colored"; women likewise.

As a small child, I was impressed and thought how neat it was to have more than just one restroom! Nothing in my young impressionable mind interpreted anything negative.

A few years later, I was playing youth baseball, as almost all young boys in this area did. Many of my teammates were black and from the northeast side of town across the tracks (railroad tracks) called the Flats. They (Niggers) all lived over there. The browns (Mexicans) lived on the northwest side. Again, I thought how neat to have your own little town.

My best friend and teammate was a great black ballplayer that we called Rabbit because he was small and so fast.

Before the season began, it was acknowledged that Rabbit did not have a birth certificate and could not validate his actual age and would not be allowed to play. My father was a big baseball fan and would stay sober long enough to coach the short summer baseball season. He so wanted Rabbit for our team that he did all the work needed and paid all expenses to get Rabbit a birth certificate so he could play on our team.

I remember we had a great and fun season. I don't remember wins or losses or our record, but I remember it was great fun.

To celebrate the fun season, my father planned for a team barbecue at our backyard with hot dogs and hamburgers. When the day arrived, my dad had me go with him in his workstation wagon to drive to the Flats to pick up some of our black teammates. I assumed it was because they didn't have their own rides.

I remember the party was great fun—everyone playing games with lots of food! I did not notice any of the adults. It had been so much fun, when I asked my father if I could invite a couple of teammates to sleep over, he quickly asked "Who?" and said yes. I was excited that my sleepover would extend the fun and that Rabbit could use one of our sleeping bags.

When the party ended, my father called for me and the black players to load up into the station wagon for the return ride home. We got to the Flats and were dropping off player after player when we stopped at Rabbit's house.

My father told Rabbit to get out and go on home. I thought there had been a mistake and told my father, "No, he's spending the night with us!" Rabbit left our car and went home, and my father told me, "*They* live over here." I was very disappointed and confused as we drove home, and I found *all* of my teammates had left and there was to be no sleepover.

I asked why and was told, "Those people don't belong over here." Again, innocently thinking this was all a misunderstanding, I mentioned the different restrooms at the courthouse: one for whites, one for colored. I was told that was because "those people" are not as "good" as "whites" and to not ask any more questions.

For many young children, this would be the indoctrination to racism and exclusion. I did *not* see nor accept it that way. If anything, I identified with their rejection and, going forward, would watch for anyone being excluded and offer friendship.

Discipline at a friend's house

On rare occasions, even society's outcasts gather together for fellowship and fun. I remember one such occasion that also seemed to symbolize what life is like with those who are negative-cycle enslaved. You seem to have finally found a positive rhythm with everything, not necessarily going well—rather, just not going badly. Then, unexpectedly, just as you begin to trust how to live life, you get cold-cocked right upside your head! *Wham!* Where did that come from? What did I do wrong this time?

We were attending a summer cookout at the Rices'. Mr. Rice was a friend of my father and a well-known town mechanic. He, too, was an abusive alcoholic known for wife beating and family abuse. He had two sons: one my age and a friend, and one older, a friend of my older brothers.

A number of families were present and participating in the typical cookout tasks: food and drink prep, barbecue pit prep, chairs and tables, etc. Each group of adults seemed to have a regular routine. The kids in attendance ranged from babies and toddlers to high schoolers, boys and girls. The adults went about their prep and business; and the kids, as usual, knew to stay out of the way, go play, and not cause any trouble.

The routine was playing out rather well, it seemed, as dusk began giving way to darkness. Us younger kids would try to keep up with the older kids in their games and fun. The toddlers and babies were tended by some mothers and a group of children helpers who just couldn't keep up in the games or didn't enjoy being constantly picked on and made fun of.

Occasionally, the kids would get a little too loud and a little too close to the adult domino and card games or the guitar playing and be scolded and eventually warned. I—and I think everyone—specially noticed Mr. Rice. It seemed out of nowhere he would jump up and run to our group and very loudly warn his oldest son to "stop causing trouble!"

This same routine of fun and festivities continued through the night, food, desserts, and entertainment. But as aforementioned, fate would not allow us to have an uneventful celebration.

Without provocation, it seemed to every one of every group, the night exploded. Mr. Rice came running into our older-kids fun group and grabbed his oldest son and began to yell and scream at him. It seemed Mr. Rice was "fed up" with his son chasing the girls and making fun. The rest of us kids stopped playing and scattered to find our own parents and a safe space.

Mr. Rice continued with his son and began spanking him by hand as he violently tossed his son. Suddenly, Mr. Rice grabbed a water hose, bent it, and began whipping his son all over his body. His son was screaming, crying, and apologizing as he pleaded for his life.

Women began taking their children to their vehicles to leave. Some of the men began to intervene to stop the beating that had visually become serious abuse.

As I was pulled away to our car to leave, I remember seeing Mr. Rice, still yelling threats, being forcibly restrained. I, to this day, clearly remember his son seriously wailing and now filthy and blood-ied from being tossed, dragged, and whipped all over the yard. Lastly, I stared with a fixed gaze at the water hose, astonished at the pain it had inflicted from the hands of a seemingly delirious person.

Unknowingly, this scene would occur again in my later youth and in a way that haunts me to this very day!

Pedophile

C. L. Walker (Chama Lee Walker) was a Native American who served in World War II and was a veterans counselor. He had much Nazi war memorabilia that he proudly displayed. He was a very friendly, joyous person and liked by everyone.

At first, he appeared as a Boy Scout helper for our local troop and displayed plenty of outdoorsman skills. Over time, he became an assistant scoutmaster and eventually became a scoutmaster of his own troop. That he became a scoutmaster did not create any curiosity at the time, though our town was so small and participation so scarce, it barely had need of more than one Boy Scout troop.

It was quietly accepted that the creation was due to a "power struggle" and fit of jealousy between the masters. As mine, I'm sure most parents paid little attention and had little concern regarding who would babysit as long as the cost remained low.

All the scouts competed for his attention and the opportunity to be chosen by him for his special secret projects. It was kind of like a crowning of respect and accomplishment to be his chosen recruit for special tasks and priority to be close by his side or be chosen to sleep in his tent on weekend campouts or ride in his car while traveling to events, especially in the front seat.

Unexpectedly, many scouts had their trust seriously violated. Beer, naked posing, photos, and eventually, "manly grab-ass tomfoolery" touching.

Upon reporting such occurrence to my mother, I was scolded for "making up" such serious nonsense and told to "hush and don't say another word about it to anyone."

I never again was in his tent or car or alone with him.

Remember, the circumstances of your life do not define you. How you react to your circumstances does define you!

Chapter 1

My Lifestyle Cycle of Dysfunction!

I was born to a dysfunctional and abusive family. With no caring positive mentor, no good things developed my life.

On April 21, 1970, I wrote the following:

I Am God's Error

Life is a farce that is taken for granted,
By those who've not lived a life of the dead.
One whose existence was one of God's error,
Is one whose life history must never be read.
My life has the omens of Satan's forgiveness.
It's death given life—a life that can't die.
I'm doomed to live on in this stage of reflection
And no one is willing to give a reply.
The question I yearn to have answered and ended,
The question is simple:
The question is "Why?"

My memories include a family life of drunkenness, beatings, destruction, and violence by a father of multiple marriages with one disabled, bedridden half brother, a mother of many marriages, grandparents of divorce and multiple marriages, two full brothers, and one oldest half sister—each demonstrating a life cycle of sin, promiscuity, abuse, divorce, abandonment.

My childhood memories are of loneliness, emptiness, fear, no love, and no hope. We were poor, seldom had supervision. Our friends were of similar despair: trouble, alcoholism, drugs, crime. Life was a void.

Being the youngest, I generally ran around with or was allowed to tag along with older friends of my siblings and was introduced to their influence of trouble at a much earlier age.

I had plenty of girlfriends growing up and went steady starting in fifth grade. Going steady never really worked out well for me. The girls thought I was overly shy since I never showed up for the movies, or when I did, I didn't sit with my girlfriend (which didn't go over very well). Because of my hearing impairment, I could not hear quite intimate talk or whispers, especially in loud surroundings. The impairment caused me many social rejections and exclusions throughout my life.

The hearing deficiency also created learning difficulties at school, but I had no problems with grades. I was smart enough to make any grade I desired. I just never experienced a motivation or reward that proved worth the effort. I could even plan my three-day school expulsions to fulfill my own calendar desires. The teachers and counselor were never concerned. They provided their spare time for the other students that showed potential. I was determined to graduate high school and not be like the real losers.

Later in life, the hearing loss kept me from being drafted for the Viet Nam War. I did not reveal the loss in advance because I wanted to be drafted so I could get out of my dysfunctional living environment. I was even willing to go to Viet Nam and die.

I began working as soon as possible. With no home allowance, if I wanted anything, I had to earn it myself. In high school I took DECA (Distributive Education Clubs of America), beginning as a junior. I would be out of school by around noon and go to work at a local grocery store each afternoon into evening.

I was always a very hard worker. I learned things quickly and had a knack of common sense. Once I was given a task, I did not stop until it was completed, and it had to be the best. I was a perfectionist, which oftentimes created tremendous extra stress. Some credit for this work ethic is probably due to the few times I was forced to help in my father's painting work. He would not tolerate mistakes, sloppiness, or incompleteness. As well, my first few grocery store bosses, too, did not tolerate slackness or inefficiency. One first grocery manager did not even allow breaks, at least for the men and boys.

I believe this was the beginning of my workaholism. Throughout my adult life and professions, I consistently achieved best awards and status. At times, it became a mechanism for avoiding undesirable circumstances, as I could just bury myself in my task and prevent facing the undesired. It was an addiction that served me well and, when needed, provided me a safe place of escape.

I bought my own car with my mother cosigning. My father took a test-drive with me, out of pressure from my mother. He said it was okay, though it almost caught fire during the test-drive. Smoke billowed out from under the dashboard, and many wires' insulation were burned off. I didn't know any better and wanted it so bad, I never said a word. The car was in the high school auto mechanics shop having an engine overhaul within six months. So I was making car payments but not driving. Overall, the two-door Chevy Impala with bucket seats and Fenton 500 three-speed floor shifter was quite attractive (though not fast, which was probably an unknown blessing).

Once I had a car, loneliness was no longer a problem, and I even, at times, had girlfriends in various close towns. One-on-one in a car was never a problem, and the back seat was very comfortable. I had plenty of sexual activity and was even engaged—with ring and all—while a senior in high school, but the unhappiness and inner void never went away. Companionship is not the same as real friends or love.

I found myself, more and more, depending on alcohol and drugs to face the next day, to get through the day, to finish the day, to forget, yet always haunted by just that. What I wanted to forget was my everyday life, but the nightmare never ended. Every time I awoke, it started again!

Life was school, work, Dairy Queen, bootleggers, drag Main Street, and parties, but that never completely filled the personal void or provided hope for the long-term cycles, habits, and addictions.

Chapter 2

Snapped

As a junior in high school, I came home drunk again late one night. Upon entering home, I saw my father lying drunk in bed as so many times previously. All the terrifying memories of my childhood came rushing into my mind—reliving themselves, torturing me again.

Mentally I *snapped!*

I pulled him out of bed. I beat him. I dragged him into the backyard, beating him. I tied him to a light pole. I beat him with a *garden hose* to finally punish him for all his abuse to my mother and the many years when I was too small to help her, for which she had begged and scolded us. I felt fulfilled, vindicated. I felt I was no longer a disappointment to my mother. I felt I had broken all the cycles!

But upon hearing considerable yelling, I turned to see and heard my mother at the back door yelling *at me* to *stop* because *I had become just like my father!*

I stopped, I was confused, I was disillusioned, I was shocked, I was empty, and somehow, my mother was saying it was my fault.

I had come full *cycle*; I had become my father! There was no *hope!*

I got in my car and left. I drove to the bootlegger and purchased beer.

I wanted escape. I wanted to get away. I wanted to be loved. I wanted to die! I drove to a familiar drinking spot, intending to drink and then commit suicide.

I obviously fell asleep.

Upon awakening the next morning, I started the cycle and routine over, but this time, as a very broken soul wandering without purpose and *no hope*!

I had lost out to my cycle, habit, addiction.

Chapter 3

The Beginning of Change

I met a party friend's Colorado cousin: homecoming queen, blonde, beautiful, college student who didn't curse, smoke, drink, or do drugs. I knew immediately I was going to be with her. A total opposite; I'll never understand the attraction.

She would visit almost every weekend after that. We would attend parties together, each being ourselves—she, near perfect; I, just wild! It temporarily filled my void; it gave me temporary happiness, some hope. Someone loved being with me (or at least the fun and chaos), but the weekday absence was almost too much to bear.

New Beginnings

I now had a better job doing data processing at the Sudan Feed Lot run by Mr. Jim Davidson, a man who saw something in me he thought was good and potential.

I left the job against his advice and offer and moved to Amarillo so I could start business school (I was always in a hurry and thought

I could prove myself if given a chance, and those schools will enroll anyone if you can make the payments) and so I could be near her daily.

I was finally away from all my dysfunctional family and environment. My void seemed filled. I finally had someone who loved me into marriage. But through the continued partying and drinking and my imperfectness, the emptiness and worry of abandonment would creep in and create unhappiness and distrust. It was a new style of unhappiness. Our differences created a divide and unhappiness, beginning a new void and continuing my cycle.

Having a chance to visit her perfect, loving family in Colorado during a school break, we also visited Denver. We fell in love with the beautiful city, and upon leaving, I secured a grocery store job beginning in two weeks.

We rushed home, made arrangements, packed, and moved to Denver, 550 miles away from *all* my haunting dysfunction—family and environment.

She could finish school in Denver, and there were many more job opportunities. I had a grocery store job making more than double my current wage, and my school would transfer. A new beginning for sure! *Real hope!*

But through the continued drinking with my new workmates, trying to fit in, and my imperfectness, the arguing and worry would creep in and create unhappiness and distrust. It was again a new style of unhappiness and continuation of my cycle.

We were going to have a baby, a son. I just knew that would be the final answer to happiness and being fulfilled. We would finally have and be that perfect family like hers.

It did not. I was miserable and dreaded coming home. Unhappy, an empty void, no reason to live, except for my child. It would not be fair that I be cheated out of this creation—a continued cycle. Again, no hope!

Chapter 4

Visitors at the Door

Late one afternoon, two visitors came to the door and introduced themselves as from the "little church a couple of blocks over." I told them to wait while I called my wife to the door, as I was not interested in talking to them, for they had nothing of interest to me.

Church, on the few occasions I could remember attending, had never had anything that interested, motivated, or captured my attention. On the contrary, my memories were of embarrassment, disillusionment, or outright pious rejection.

As a child, it was obvious my clothes did not meet the "standard" for that venue. There was embarrassment and snickering by those other little "Christian" members.

Being told to sit in the back of the special services (Christmas, Easter) so the nicely dressed children members could be upfront was a tearful memory.

In such a small community, where everyone knows everyone else's business, it is devastating to have anyone, but especially the "righteous," shake their heads quietly and write you off as having "no hope for someone like you!" Sadly, the Pharisees were alive and well.

As an adult, upon any visit, it was surely and obviously a cold shoulder when no one even ventured to provide a greeting and avoided eye contact. Even at one point, our babysitter's husband told me bluntly to my face I would not be accepted at his church because my hair was too long!

I believed there was a God and, through my early dysfunctional family life, had many times yelled questions to him without replies, answers, or comfort. I believed Jesus was a loving revolutionary that was counterculture. I identified with his underdog status. I believed he was truly love immaculate in his day.

Curiosity

Toward the end of the following week, my wife sheepishly approached me. She asked if we could attend the final revival church service of that week at that church our previous week's visitors had invited her.

Any previous such discussion or dialogue would have caused a disrupting argument and ruin of the evening. I did not want the day to be ruined, so I surprised her with agreement, figuring a service at such a small church could not last that long and would help her overcome her such periodic "spiritual spasm."

Upon entering the tiny church, to my recollection, we were directed to the nursery for our two-year-old son. Returning to the sanctuary, we entered the small room of three aisles with worn long wooden pews covered by worn pew-length crimson velvet cushions. Many of the back pews were roped off to supposedly force the attendees to sit closer to the front.

The rope caused me no restraint. I removed it and entered a far pew to the left. We sat about midway in what was to be an otherwise empty pew. I surveyed the interior to be aware of the exit route.

Strange turn of events

After a bit of old hymnal singing, a pastor of Victoria Baptist Church of Vancouver, British Columbia, Canada, walked to the pulpit and began talking. Surprisingly, he was a young man with a smile. My attention had been captured.

The speaker surprised me, as I had expected a long, boring sermon from old, front-to-end Bible verses delivered with heavy brows. It was nothing of the sort. He told the story of Jesus Christ, supposedly the loving son of God, who, out of his love, sacrificed himself for *me* to provide an opportunity to accept God's eternal forgiveness and love and abundant life.

This was a story I had never fully heard. I thought only one person loved me.

Chapter 5

The Story

This tale said God had created everything and everyone, and "it was good." God loved everyone so much, he gave them the ultimate free will. This was his real gift to see if they would, in turn, love him. His gift to us was life. Our gift to him would be what we would do with that life.

As mankind evolved and demonstrated their selfishness, a sinful self-nature in contrast to God's love, God provided laws and sacred scriptures inspired to his chosen prophets as guidance to assist them. The laws may have helped some, but it was also complicated as mankind continued to repeat their own selfish cycle.

Eventually, God realized mankind's opportunity to demonstrate their love for him should be simplified. God loves us so much, he would send his own Son in person to explain to mankind his available love, gift of redemption, and abundant eternal life.

By repenting, turning from our selfishness and accepting Jesus as God's son, he will, as our Savior, redeem us from our sins and allow us to become an eternal blessed member of his eternity to share an abundant life of joy, breaking out of our cycle of sin, disappointment, and sadness, securing our only true hope!

Politics

Unfortunately, at this time, God's chosen people were oppressed by the foreign conquering Roman government. The local governing Roman officials were generally unhappy being away from their own desirable homeland in such a harsh climate, forced to govern an unruly population of different culture. The Romans wanted and demanded the least resistance possible and provided as much punishment and discipline needed.

The local population, too, were unhappy with the foreign dominance, taxation, and lack of respect, but were not powerful enough to revolt. They were inspired by the prophets' message of a coming Messiah, who, as their King, would one day free them from their unjust rule and domination.

Jesus began his ministry sharing God's love and deliverance from domination to God's new earthly kingdom. As Scripture recorded, throughout the land, Jesus shared God's love and performed many miracles, demonstrating God's power and love.

Unfortunately, the local religious leaders became jealous and envious of Jesus's growing following and popularity and did not accept him as God's actual son, but merely as just another "voice from the wilderness." They selfishly feared their own loss of popularity and power.

Likewise, the current local Roman rulers feared a possible revolt by a rumored "new King of the Jews." Such tension would reflect poorly on their leadership to the home Roman government.

The jealous religious leaders would quietly and secretively plot with the Roman authorities to solve both concerns by having the Romans crucify Jesus and end his threats and protect their own positions.

Trial and crucifixion

In the darkest of night, the Roman soldiers were led to the Mount of Olives and the Garden of Gethsemane, where Jesus was praying with his disciples. Jesus knew his destiny and sacrifice and was praying so intensely to God his Father, "drops of sweat fell from his brow like blood."

The soldiers arrested Jesus, tied him, and took him away to the higher Roman authorities. The Jewish leaders insisted the Romans execute Jesus for breaking their laws and so his followers would blame the Romans and not them.

The Roman authorities sent Jesus back and forth among themselves as they could find no fault, nor did they want to be associated with this injustice or of provoking trouble.

Pilate, the Roman ruler, saw that there was nothing he could do to make the people change their minds. In fact, it looked as if there would be a riot. So he took some water and washed his hands in front of them all. He said, "I am not guilty of this man's death. You are the ones who are doing it!"

Since the locals had no authority to execute people, it would require Romans to fulfill such sentencing. Because Jesus was proclaimed to be the new King of the Jews, he could be deemed a threat to Roman rule and thereby executed. The Romans reluctantly agreed to perform the execution.

The soldiers took Jesus away tied. They covered his eyes so that he could not see them. Then they hit him and mocked, "Be a prophet and tell us who hit you!" And they shouted all kinds of insults and laughed at him.

They gave him thirty-nine lashes, as forty lashes was supposed to assure death from a cat-o'-nine-tails. A cat-o'-nine-tails is a whip. It consists of nine pieces of cord or leather strands, each tied with a series of knots with pieces of metal and rock. The device traditionally punished prisoners by whipping their bare backs and ripping off their skin.

The soldiers made a crown from thorny branches and gouged it onto Jesus's head until blood dripped. Then they put a purple robe around him. They kept coming up to him and saying, "Hail to the king of the Jews!" And they hit him in the face. They spit on him. Then they took a stick and kept hitting him on the head.

Jesus was forced to carry his own cross down the Via Dolorosa, Path of Sorrow, to Golgotha, the Place of the Skull, a barren hill of execution. There they laid Jesus onto the cross and drove spikes through his hands and feet into the rugged cross. Once nailed, the cross was uplifted and forcefully dropped into a hole to stand erect for display with another convicted criminal crucified on each side. The weight of the hanging body would eventually cause a prisoner to suffocate. Often, their legs would be broken to prevent any sustained support, prolonging suffering.

The soldiers laughed at Jesus and made fun of him. There was a jar full of sour wine there, so the soldiers soaked a sponge in it. They put the sponge on a branch of a hyssop plant and lifted it to Jesus's mouth. When he tasted the wine, he said, "It is finished." Then he bowed his head and died.

The soldiers then took his clothes and, by rolling dice, divided these among themselves. Then they bowed down on their knees and pretended to honor him as a king.

The next day was a special Sabbath day. The Jewish leaders did not want the body to stay on the cross on the Sabbath day. So they asked Pilate to order that the legs of the criminals be broken to hasten their death, and they asked that the bodies be taken down from the crosses. But when the soldiers came close to Jesus, they saw that he was already dead. So they did not break his legs. But one of the soldiers stuck his spear into Jesus's side. Immediately blood and water poured out.

Jesus, as his Father commanded, sacrificed himself to provide the sinners of the world a free gift offer of redemption, salvation. "For God so loved the world, He gave His only Son, that whoever believes and accepts Him as God's Son and their Savior will not perish (be separated from God), but will have eternal life in Heaven" with them. For God did not send his Son into the world to condemn the world, but to save the world through him. He offered this as a free gift, unable to be earned.

The church speaker startled me as he added, "For God so loved *you.*"

Had Jesus been a mere man, his death on the cross would be the end of this story. Jesus would be just another tale of a kind person trying to do good, but he *was not!*

Jesus's body was laid wrapped in a borrowed tomb to await the traditional burial preparation. Three days later, women went to the tomb for the preparation, only to find the body missing and the tomb empty.

Jesus had risen and would appear to the women, his disciples, and thousands of others before rising to heaven to be with God our Father. He will await there until the appointed time of God when he will return here to establish his new earthly kingdom. In the meantime, as his followers, we are to spread his story, news, and invitation for everyone.

Chapter 6

You Must "Take It Personal"

The little church then began playing a hymn of invitation, inviting people to come forward to accept Jesus as their Savior. Standing, playing music, and singing for what seemed an eternity.

I stood there gripping the pew in front of me, struggling to understand the emotion I was experiencing. The speaker said God loved *me* so much he sacrificed his only Son to offer me the opportunity to be forgiven, excused, and become a heavenly part of God's family!

Only one person loved me. I was not worthy of a Savior's love and sacrifice. I could not live such a Christian life or be part of such a group. I was not worthy, and it was not altogether my fault!

I planned my escape to exit this aisle, turn right, sprint down that main aisle, and out that door to my car. I thought the message was too good to be true, especially for someone like me, while sad, torturous memories flooded my mind.

Startling and making my dilemma even worse, my wife left me there alone and walked down the aisle to the front of the church.

Now I struggled by myself, more alone than I had ever been in my entire life. Why had everyone forsaken me?

The music seemed to play on continually, but I felt I could wait long enough to escape. I knew I was not good enough to accept this invitation and gift. Just as soon as I thought that exact thought, the speaker again came to the microphone and seemingly stated directly to me, "Don't let anything keep you from taking that first step. Jesus loves *you*!"

I walked to the end of the aisle. I looked to the right and the sanctuary exit, but I knew that direction provided no hope. I looked to the left, to the front of the church, where it seemed everyone was standing, smiling, waiting to welcome me into God's family. There seemed to be hope awaiting me.

What then seemed like quite an eternity passed, until I turned left, went forward, and started my new forgiven life in Jesus Christ, once and for all breaking my *cycle*!

To be saved from your sin, you must do these things:

1. meaningfully ask forgiveness for your sins;
2. be willing to turn from your sins (repent/stop doing it);
3. believe that Jesus Christ—our Lord and Savior—died for your sins and rose again.

You can accept Jesus Christ as your Savior and personal Lord by praying and meaning the following prayer:

Dear Lord Jesus,

I know I am a sinner, and I ask for your forgiveness. I believe Jesus died for my sins and rose from the dead. I trust and follow you as my Savior and the Lord and Master of my life. Guide my life and help me do your will and become the Christian you want me to be.

In Jesus's name, amen.

If you pray this prayer and accept Jesus Christ as your personal Savior and Lord of your life or have questions, concerns or seek help, please contact us (Goddoesloveyou777@gmail.com) so we can congratulate you and offer you encouragement. You are loved, and we care!

Chapter 7

What Do You Do Next?

The next day, my life was perfect, without care, worry, or problem, right?

Wrong!

I had to go back to my regular life of work and school and family. I knew something was greatly different though, but I was rapidly becoming confused. Even my drinking, cursing friends noticed my difference.

I did not deny my difference, but also I could not explain it. I knew I was no longer the same person on the inside. It was like I had experienced a rebirth!

> Jesus answered, "I assure you, everyone must be born again/born from above. Anyone who is not born again cannot be in God's kingdom. (John 3:3 ERV)

When anyone belongs to Christ, they become a new person. Their old way of life has gone. Their new life has begun! All this is what God does for us. Because of what Christ has done, God has brought us back to himself as his friends. Now he wants us to bring other people to be his friends too. *That is the job that he has given to us.*

God's message is this: "By Christ's death, God was bringing people of the world back to himself, as his friends. He would no longer keep their sins in his thoughts" (2 Corinthians 5:17–19 ERV).

That is the message that God wants us to tell people.

Then how do we learn to do this?

On the outside, I needed help and guidance. I could not break my old habits, addictions by myself.

As a newborn baby, we all begin our growth consuming simple but wholesome nourishment: milk. Solids and meats come later. We do not run before we practice and learn to crawl and toddle.

If you were motivated by an Olympic marathon medalist and wanted to emulate that success, you would not immediately enter a marathon. If so, you would fail miserably, be humiliated, and could suffer injury.

You would seek a trainer, a mentor to guide and pace you. Step-by-step you would learn the basics and adjust your life accordingly. Slowly, even with possible setbacks, you would achieve successes and rewards until it became a natural way of life for you. Then you might even begin mentoring/discipling another interested person.

You need to break from one cycle and form a new, more rewarding cycle!

Your new life in Jesus Christ is the same. You first need proper perspective of your new life's meaning and purpose.

God's will and plan for your new life

> Jesus said, "I came that they may have life and have it abundantly. My purpose is to give them a rich and satisfying life." (John 10:10)

What must we do to gain this abundant life?

There are only *two* commands! These are the two new laws/commandments/guides God gave us:

This is the great and *first* commandment.

> And he said, "You shall love the *One* and Only Lord your God with all your heart, and with all your soul, and with all your mind.
>
> And the *second* is this: you shall love your neighbor as yourself.
>
> The entire law and all the demands of the prophets are based on these two commandments." (Matthew 22:36–40)

To make God's love fully effective in your life, do the following:

- *Stop sinning.*

  If I'm a Christian (saved) and keep sinning, will God turn away from me?

It's true that sin puts up a barrier between us and God and cuts us off from the fellowship He wants us to have with Him. The Bible says, "But your iniquities [sins] have separated you from your God; your sins have hidden His face from you, so that He will not hear" (Isaiah 59:2). (Franklin Graham)

But that doesn't mean God refuses to have anything to do with us.

Don't let sin come between you and God. God loves you, and Christ died to take away our sins.

When we do sin, however, we need to confess/admit it and seek God's forgiveness at once.

- *Choose to practice his teachings for the rest of your life.*

Teach me your way, O Lord; lead me in a straight path. (Psalm 27:11)

Seek His will in all you do, and He will show you which path to take. (Proverbs 3:6)

In view of this, I also do my best to maintain always a blameless conscience both before God and before men. (Acts 24:16)

- *Pray (talk to God).*

In those days when you pray, I will listen. If you look for Me in earnest, you will find Me when you seek Me. (Jeremiah 29:12, 13)

The earnest prayer of a righteous person has great power and wonderful results. (James 5:16)

If you need wisdom—if you want to know what God wants you to do—ask Him (talk to Him, pray), and He will gladly tell you. He will not resent your asking. (James 1:5)

- *Read and study the Bible*

Jesus said, "If you abide (spend time) in My word (Bible), you are My disciples (believers) indeed. And you shall know the truth, and the truth shall make you free." (John 8:31–32)

His delight is in the Lord's instruction (Bible), and he meditates (studies) on it day and night. (Psalm 1:2)

You shall meditate (study, think deeply) in it (the Bible) day and night, that you may observe to do according to all that is written in it. For then you will make your way prosperous, and then you will have good success. (Joshua 1:8)

Jesus replied: "If anyone loves Me He will cherish my word; my Father will love him and

We will come to him and make him Ours." (John 14:23–24)

All Scripture is given by inspiration of God, and is profitable for doctrine (learning), for reproof, for correction, for instruction in righteousness, that the man of God may be complete, thoroughly equipped for every good work. (2 Timothy 3:16–17)

- *Memorize the Bible*

I will delight in your statutes (written instruction); I will not forget your word (memorize). (Psalm 119:6)

My son, be attentive to My words; incline your ear to My sayings. Let them not escape from your sight; keep them within your heart. (Proverbs 4:20–21)

Guard My words as your most precious possession. Write them down and also keep them deep within your heart. (Proverbs 7:2)

- *Learn the Bible together with other believers (God's church)*

In the church, God has appointed…teachers. (1 Corinthians 12:28)

Where two or three are gathered together in My name, I am there in the midst of them. (Matthew 18:20)

Join together in following my example, brothers and sisters, and just as you have us as a model, keep your eyes on those who live as we do. (Philippians 3:17)

And let us not neglect our meeting together…but encourage one another. (Hebrews 10:25)

- *Fellowship with the believers (God's church): Acts 2:42–47.*

They devoted themselves to the apostles' teaching and to fellowship together, to the breaking of bread and to prayer. All the believers were together and had everything in common. Every day they continued to meet together in the temple courts. They broke bread in their homes and ate together with glad and sincere hearts, praising God and enjoying the favor of all the people. And the Lord added to their number daily those who were being saved.

- *Tell others about Jesus Christ.*

Go home to your friends and tell them how much the Lord has done for you and how He has had mercy on you. (Mark 5:19)

Therefore, go and make disciples (followers of Jesus) of all the nations, baptizing them in the name of the Father and the Son and the Holy Spirit. (Matthew 28:19)

But how can they call on Him to save them unless they believe in Him? And how can they believe in Him if they have never heard about Him? And how can they hear about Him unless someone tells them? (Romans 10:14)

- *Be baptized.*

    Note: Being baptized is *not* required to go to heaven, but it is a sign of obedience to God and a way of publicly declaring your decision to follow Christ.

    By being baptized, we were buried with Christ into his death. Christ has been raised from the dead by the Father's glory. And like Christ we also can live a new life. (Romans 6:4)

    Then, go and make disciples (followers of Jesus) of all the nations (everyone), baptizing them in the name of the Father and the Son and the Holy Spirit. (Matthew 28:19)

- *Demonstrate your faith in Jesus.*

    Your word (Bible scripture) is a lamp to guide my feet and a light (guide) for my path. (Psalm 119:105)

    But don't just listen to God's word. You must *do* what God's Word says. (James 1:22)

- *Do not be yoked (partnered, married, etc.) together with unbelievers.*

   Righteousness and wickedness have nothing in common and cause each other conflict (2 Corinthians 6:14).

   God's message and instructions for us were passed directly to his chosen messengers. This set of personalized messages and life instructions, as listed above, is the Bible. It is God's "instruction manual."

   The more you study and practice, the greater your understanding and benefits; the less effort, the greater your lack of understanding, confusion, and failure.

   As his instructions/stories illustrate, we need someone to walk alongside us to show us the way.

   We, too, need to grow enough to walk alongside someone else in need.

Chapter 8

Where's the Help?

Cycle, habit, or addiction? Related, cause or effect? Expert opinion will vary, differ, argue, and disagree. *Regardless, the cure, remedy, and path to change is the same and does not differ—the saving grace and lifesaving and changing love of Jesus Christ.*

The Bible

There are many translations of the Bible. In your new Christian growth, like a newborn baby begins its life on nourishing milk before solid food, you need an easy-to-read and understand Bible. Heavy-duty study Bibles can come later when you have the adequate spiritual growth. Again, this is not the time to enter a "marathon."

A group of Jesus Christ–worshiping followers

As stated in God's instructional scriptures/instructions, we need to be with experienced Jesus-loving people. Groups of these experienced believers are referred to as God's church. They are not a building, they are a group of Jesus believers that share their experience/testimony in their Savior Jesus. They seek a continually growing relationship with Jesus.

They are not a religion; they are a living relationship. They may become organized, but first and foremost, they seek the ever-growing Jesus relationship. (See "Relationship, not Religion"!)

Christian organizations

There are many groups who offer services, guidance, and help. Be sure your groups have Jesus as their foundation, not just a helping step.

One of my favorite organizations that I have personally worked with is the following:

> New Beginnings Recovery Center: Mary Brewer, Director
>
> *An Addiction Treatment Model that Builds Foundations in Bedrock*™
>
> Everything we do in our treatment program is dedicated to giving our clients a new life by healing the mind body and spirit. By providing a fully integrated addiction treatment regime you

can break the cycle of addiction and change your behavior.

www.newbeginningsrecoverydenver.com

Email: mary@nbr-services.com

Other help

Jim's story:

How I Found God's Love—Breaking the Cycle
https://youtu.be/Zppq0E1nRW0

God Does Love You
http://goddoesloveyou.wixsite.com/godlovesyou

What Do I Do Next?
http://goddoesloveyou.wixsite.com/godlovesyou/what-next

Why the Bible?
http://goddoesloveyou.wixsite.com/godlovesyou/why-the-bible

Why Jesus?
http://goddoesloveyou.wixsite.com/godlovesyou/why-jesus

What Happens When I Die?
http://goddoesloveyou.wixsite.com/godlovesyou/
what-happens-when-i-die

Don't Good People Go to Heaven?
http://goddoesloveyou.wixsite.com/godlovesyou/
dont-good-people-go-to-heaven

Why Do Bad Things Happen?
http://goddoesloveyou.wixsite.com/godlovesyou/
why-do-bad-things-happen

Why Did I Lose My Child/Baby?
https://goddoesloveyou.wixsite.com/godlovesyou/
why-did-i-lose-my-childbaby

Can I Lose My Salvation?
http://goddoesloveyou.wixsite.com/godlovesyou/
can-i-lose-my-salvation

Twitter:

God Does Love You
https://twitter.com/GodDoesLoveYou7

Facebook:
https://www.facebook.com/YesGodLovesYou/

Pinterest:
http://www.pinterest.com/goddoes/

Answers to Your Questions
http://pinterest.com/questionanswer

Facebook:
https://www.facebook.com/Answers-to-Your-Questions-17084494793367992/

Other highly recommended sources of help

Billy Graham Evangelistic Association
Franklin Graham
Samaritan's Purse
Crusade for Christ
Christian Broadcasting Network
Sports Spectrum
Fellowship of Christian Athletes
Athletes of Christ
ChristianRunners.org
All in Men: Christian Sports International
Focus on the Family
Campus Crusade for Christ
Books for Development: Libraries in Kenya
John Foundation: India
Church Under the Bridge (CUB): San Antonio, Texas
Polished Man

Habitat for Humanity

YouVersion Online Bible

GodTube.com

GodVine.com

God TV

PureFlick.com

God Tools

BibleHub.com

Chapter 9

Why Jesus?

People often ask, "What makes Jesus different from all the other religious leaders who ever lived?"

The Bible—God's authoritative word—makes it very clear that Jesus was more than just another religious teacher or prophet. It tells us instead that Jesus was unique.

He was unique in his person.

He wasn't just an unusually spiritual individual. He was more than that; he was God in human flesh. Yes, he was fully man, but he was also fully God. The Bible puts it this way: "For in Christ all the fullness of the Deity lives in bodily form."

Jesus was unique in his purpose.

Why did he come to earth? He came for one reason: to save us from our sins. As Jesus himself said, "For the Son of Man came to seek and to save what was lost" (Luke 19:10).

He did this by becoming the final sacrifice for our sins through his death on the cross. We know his promise of eternal life is true because he did something no other person has ever done: he rose from the dead—what we call the resurrection—and still lives today.

(Billy Graham Evangelistic Association, http://goingfarther. jesus.net/basics-of-christianity/)

Chapter 10

Relationship, Not Religion

God, Jesus, and the Holy Spirit are the Trinity, or three parts of God. They are not an organization or a religion.

God loves you and offers you an eternity in his perfect heaven. God gave you life and free will in hopes that you will help introduce others to Jesus as their Savior. His gift to you is life; what you do with your life is your gift to him.

God did not create religion. Religion was created by mankind, which was man's attempt to reach God. Jesus is not interested in religion and is reaching out to you. He is interested in an ongoing relationship with you.

Other religious leaders tell people, "Follow me, and I'll show you how to find truth."

Jesus says, "I am the truth" (John 14:6).

Other religious leaders tell people, "Follow me, and I'll show you the way to salvation."

Jesus says, "I am the way to eternal life" (John 14:6).

Other religious leaders tell people, "Follow me, and I'll show you how to become enlightened."

Jesus says, "I am the light of the world" (John 8:12).

Other religious leaders tell people, "Follow me, and I'll show you many doors that lead to God."

Jesus says, "I am the door" (John 10:9).

All religions are based on you doing something to earn the favor of God.

These are the attempts of people to reach God.

Christianity is based on what Christ has done for us on the cross.

Christianity is God reaching out to us.

Christianity is not a religion; it is a way of life, it is a relationship with God.

Only Jesus—because he is the unique and perfect Son of God—is qualified to offer himself as payment for our wrongdoing.

No leader of any other major religion even pretends to be able to do that.

Moses could meditate on the law.

Mohammed could brandish a sword.

Buddha could give personal counsel.

Confucius could offer wise sayings.

But none of these men were qualified to offer an atonement for the sins of the world.

Example of personal works versus God's forgiving grace: Buddha tells a parable of an errant son who became rebellious and left home, later to recognize his error and return home. The errant son is required to work off the penalty of his past misdeeds by spending years in servitude.

Jesus Christ's prodigal son leaves home and sins, but returns home to a warm welcome, celebration, and undeserved forgiveness: grace (Luke 15:11–32).

God's grace offers you redemption, not man's personal effort or works.

(Lee Strobel, *God's Outrageous Claims*)

Chapter 11

What Is My Purpose?

Where did I come from?

Just as God created the earth as a place for you to live and gain experience, he created you and gave you a body of flesh and blood in the likeness of his glorified body.

In the Old Testament, God said, "Let us make man in our own image, after our likeness" (Genesis 1:26).

Jacob declared that he had seen God face-to-face (Genesis 32:30).

Moses also spoke with God face-to-face, as a man speaks unto his friend (Exodus 33:11).

In the New Testament, when the resurrected Christ appeared to his apostles, he told them, "Handle me, and see; for a spirit has not flesh and bones, as ye see me have" (Luke 24:39).

Why did God create me?

First, he didn't make us because he was lonely. Long before we were here, God already had company with his Son and the Holy Spirit, referred to in Genesis 1:26, "Let us make man in our own image."

Second, despite not needing us, God chose to create us anyway, out of his great love: "I have loved you with an everlasting love" (Jeremiah 31:3). Yes, God loved us before he even created us. It's impossible to get our heads around that idea, but it's true; that's what everlasting love means.

Third, God created us to fulfill his eternal plan.

God, in his infinite wisdom, chose to make us a part of his eternal plan.

God is love, and because of that love and his wonderful creativity, he made us so we can enjoy all that he is and all that he's done.

> For everything comes from Him and exists
> by His power and is *intended for His glory*.
> (Romans 11:36)
>
> You are worthy, O Lord, to receive glory
> and honor and power: for You have created all
> things, and *for your glory they are and were created*.
> (Revelation 4:11)
>
> Bring all who claim me as their God, for I
> have *made them for My glory*. It was I who created
> them. (Isaiah 43:7)

What is my purpose?

God created us to glorify him and to enjoy him forever.

We were created by him and for him. He did not need us because he was lonely or wanted someone to talk to. God is perfect and complete and has always been that way. We belong completely to him. Because of that, we are to glorify him in everything that we do.

> And whatever you do, *in word and action, do everything in the name of the Lord Jesus*, giving thanks to God the Father through him. (Colossians 3:17)
>
> So whether you eat or drink or whatever you do, *do it all for the glory (honor and respect) of God.* (1 Corinthians 10:31)

How do we do that (glorify God)?

We love him, obey him, believe in Jesus Christ, trust in Jesus, receiving the free gift of salvation Jesus offers us and tell others. Only then will we give glory to God, and only then we will be able to enjoy him forever, for all eternity!

> For we are God's creation. He has created us new in Christ Jesus, *so we can do the good things he planned for us.* (Ephesians 2:10)

Perhaps the most important part we play in God's eternal plan is to point people to eternal life with God—through his Son Jesus Christ.

The Bible calls this our "ministry of reconciliation," telling others about salvation through Jesus Christ.

> And all things are of God, who reconciled (restored friendly relationship) us to Himself through Jesus Christ, and *did give to us the ministration (duty) of the reconciliation of others (restoring that relationship with others)*…and having put in us the word of the reconciliation, in behalf of Christ, then, *we are His ambassadors (chosen representatives), as if God were calling through us*, in behalf of Christ. (2 Corinthians 5:18–19)

(http://goingfarther.jesus.net/basics-of-christianity/)

Chapter 12

What God Has Done in My Life

I was born to a dysfunctional and abusive family. My memories are a family life of drunkenness, beatings, destruction, and violence by a father of multiple marriages, with one disabled, bedridden half brother, a mother of many marriages, grandparents of divorce and multiple marriages, two full brothers, and one oldest half sister—each demonstrating a life cycle of sin, promiscuity, abuse, divorce, abandonment. With no caring positive mentor, no good things developed my life (http://jimiveymsm.wix.com/jamesivey).

On April 21, 1970, I wrote the following:

I Am God's Error

Life is a farce that is taken for granted,
By those who've not lived a life of the dead.
One whose existence was one of God's error,
Is one whose life history must never be read.
My life has the omens of Satan's forgiveness.

It's death given life—a life that can't die.
I'm doomed to live on in this stage of reflection
And no one is willing to give a reply.
The question I yearn to have answered and ended,
The question is simple:
The question is "Why?"

But we are not born bad or evil, and regardless of our different circumstances, we are made by a loving God. He loves us and wants a relationship with us. He wants to give us an abundant life!

Making your way in the world today
Takes everything you've got,
Taking a break from all your worries
Sure would help a lot!
Wouldn't you like to get away?
...
Sometimes you want to go
Where everybody knows your name
And they're always glad you came

You want to be where you can see
Our troubles are all the same.
You want to be where everybody knows your name.

Cheers
Source: Musixmatch
Songwriters: Portnoy Gary/Angelo Judy Hart

And alas, miracles truly do happen, and God has meaning and purpose for each person's life.

In 1974, I wrote the following:

Faith

There once was a time I felt like hell,
My life was so empty I crawled in a shell.
I had nowhere to turn, and wanted to die.
What's so strange was…I didn't know why.
I was confused and out of my mind,
I just couldn't leave my problems behind,
But then one day to my surprise,
I found someone who told me no lies.
She was always there and she listened to me;
She showed me a life I thought never could be.
She turned me toward God, and that helped a lot;
And that is a lesson I've never forgot
She gave birth to me a life all wonderful and new;
Now, I'm alive and so happy,
Claudia, my faith is you!

Now, as a believer in Jesus Christ and layperson, I owe all my happiness, success, blessings, and salvation to Jesus Christ, who I accepted as my Savior one week before Easter 1974 at Calvary Baptist Church of Englewood, Colorado.

Over my continuing spiritual growth and journey, I have participated in fourteen lay revivals in Montana, Utah, Colorado, and Texas and have led over twenty people to salvation in Jesus Christ.

I have lived in the Denver, Colorado, area since 1971 and three years in the Pacific Northwest (Seattle).

Claudia, my wife since 1970, was a medical laboratory technician / pediatric office manager.

My sons include Jason (Connecticut), Jeremy (Colorado), and Jordan (Colorado). I have nine grandchildren; Derek James is my first grandson by Jason, and Samuel James by Jordan, named after myself, the greatest honors I have ever received.

Carson William, Connor Matthew, and Kaitlyn Nicole are also my grandchildren by Jason.

Phoenix Aiden and Landon Gabriel are my grandsons by Jeremy.

Lilah Ellen and Thomas Vady are also my youngest granddaughter and grandson by Jordan.

I have had four children named after me (Derek James [Jason], Samuel James [Jordan], Ryan James [Paula], James Curtis [Curtis]), two books dedicated to me (Cecil Moe), and one poem written about me (Fed Bapp).

I received my Masters of Scientific Management/Leadership degree (MSM) from Regis University, Denver, Colorado, and Bachelor of Science degree in business management from Metropolitan State College of Denver.

Entrepreneur

I have owned/operated my own businesses, Consult Results, Inc., Colorado Precision Transmission, Inc., Sun Transmission, Inc.

I held positions as Olympic HomeCare Products regional marketing manager, Nestle Chocolate district manager, Southland Corporation district manager, and retail manager for Allied Supermarkets.

Founder/designer/author

Online eVangelism
Founded: 2013
Internet Gospel
Fulfilling God's great commission and command

God Does Love You
http://goddoesloveyou.wix.com/godlovesyou
https://www.facebook.com/YesGodLovesYou/
http://www.pinterest.com/goddoes/

Answers to Your Questions
http://pinterest.com/questionanswer/

But how can they call on Him to save them
unless they believe in Him?
And how can they believe in Him if they
have never heard about Him?

And how can they hear about Him unless
someone tells them? (Romans 10:14)

Designer

God Does Loves You website (http://goddoesloveyou.wix.com/
godlovesyou)

God Does Loves You website (http://www.pinterest.com/
goddoes/)

Answers to Your Questions website (http://www.pinterest.com/
questionanswer)

Author

Distance Education Online Platform Development: CourseWeb

Codesigner / beta tester of CourseWeb educational platform,
NACS (National Association of College Stores), Cornell University,
Metropolitan State College of Denver

Interview article, *College Store Executive* magazine, February
1999

Major contributor to Colorado Christian University Online
Writing Lab (OWL)

Authored business articles for the Internet entertainment magazine *Diaspora*

Educator

University of Phoenix University, certified advanced facilitator, Practitioner Faculty

Colorado Christian University: Dr. Day's Official Dean's Gold Star List for Teaching Excellence! (April 2014)

Jones International University: Gold Standard Faculty, MBA academic coordinator

Denver Technical College: eBusiness Instructor of 2000, Outstanding Faculty 1998–2001

Metropolitan College of Denver: Excellence in Teaching 1997, 1996, 1995

Community College of Denver: Outstanding Faculty, Outstanding Advisor 1994

Things we do repeatedly, good or bad, can become personal choice habits. If bad enough, they can become addictions that physically control and eventually destroy us. The environmental influence of these experienced cycles of others can lead to become our repeated paths.

But there is *one* ultimate medicine, healer, that can remedy all these and provide us a path and life of abundance: Jesus.

Seek and you will find!

Afterword

Some Cannot Break Their Cycle!

My father, as I have described, was a violent, abusive alcoholic. He provided no support for any of my family for any time I have ever been aware. He did not, or could not, break out of his destructive life cycle.

Yet from an honest review, there are occasions that I am aware of and have experienced that make me believe there are some personal forces that some people cannot master or learn to control or even avoid. This, I do not believe, excuses nor condones any resulting improper behavior: drunkenness, abuse, lack of support, etc.

My family's dysfunction has caused me a life of trauma. It has severely hindered my personal growth, behavior, maturity, and opportunity. I study my behavior traits not for the purpose of blame, but to learn acknowledgment, accommodation, and repair. With such handicap and lacking caring mentoring, my life has been a true example of self-help and survival of the fittest.

My father's father was an alcoholic. His mother had unsuccessful marriages and was abusive and demonstrated hatred constantly.

She was partial, showed favoritism, and ridiculed any one or thing of which she was not pleased. She was a racist.

My father's first marriage ended in divorce with a severely brain-damaged, bedridden son, Rodney. His wife could not accept these things and left. My grandmother stepped in to supervise for my half brother because she knew my father, being the drunk he was, could not provide his needed care, though I could honestly recognize that my father truly loved and grieved for Rodney.

My mother attempted to care for Rodney but could not because of the lack of support and drunkenness of my father. I can remember as a small boy having walked home from school and entering my house to a tremendous ruckus. As I turned into a room, there were my grandmother and father having backed my mother into a corner. They were beating her for not properly caring for Rodney and being a bad mother, a traumatic scene that haunts me to this day.

My grandmother came and took Rodney away from my home and gave him to my uncle James. This uncle, one of three sons, had served in the military with an outstanding record. My grandmother paid for a home for them in a very distant location, causing much family resentment. My uncle and aunt lovingly cared for Rodney until his death.

There were numerous occasions when my father's public drunkenness resulted in legal incarcerations. These included city jail, county jail, and eventually his legal incarceration in state care hospitals.

After having spent six months in the state hospital in Wichita Falls, we visited to bring him home upon his release. He had received glowing reports of his good recovery and helpfulness with the other recovering patients. He even bragged about our upcoming new life and his upcoming family support and care. He was a very professional and respected painter and carpenter and always had work available. He, again, truly seemed to have conquered his cycle.

Unfortunately, on the long drive back to our home in West Texas and upon arrival, he already had slurred speech, clammy skin, and bloodshot eyes and an abusive attitude. At the end of one week's work, he was abusively drunk. He was haunted and recaptured by his cycle. He could not face life and responsibility.

I observed on many of these occasions—and better acknowledged later as an adult—that while incarcerated, my father, once fully sober, was a kindhearted person with a heart for helping others. In at least two of the state hospitals, he even became a trusted helper. It seemed he could escape his cycle during these incarcerations.

Down deep he had a kindness and concern that was obvious. On some occasions, before being again overwhelmed by his destructive cycle, he would even attempt to enact that good nature.

On one rare sober Thanksgiving holiday, he secretly invited both his mother and his brother and sister-in-law for the feast in an attempt to reconcile their family. As explained in "Don't Go to Grandma's House," there was a tremendous deserved hatred from my uncle and aunt toward my grandmother.

My grandmother was in the kitchen, which had a direct view to the front door, supervising the meal preparation. When my uncle and aunt arrived, they all locked eyes. My uncle rushed the kitchen and locked his hands around my grandmother's throat as they went to the floor, kicking and screaming. They were broken apart by my father, and they all departed, swearing threatening messages at each other, as well as at my father—an attempted but very failed reconciliation.

A number of years later, while living in Colorado and after my salvation, I received a phone call from a hometown family friend and pastor. He informed me that my father and local uncle had both been drunk and caused a traffic accident that hospitalized a couple. Because the accident had occurred on the state highway, my father and uncle were arrested and incarcerated in the county jail. They had been tried and found guilty of damages, and because of his long-term past and record, he would be sentenced to the state penitentiary, not state hospital.

With the help of the local pastor and agreement of my loving wife, I provided a letter to the court offering to take custody for the supervision of my father. The judge agreed, with the stipulation that my father never return to Texas (known as hillbilly justice).

My dad was provided his own private bedroom in my home. I told him that in his room was his privacy and that he could drink himself to death if he desired, but that on Sundays, we would go to church. He promised not to smoke, drink, or curse in front of my infant son.

For his time with us, as in his previous incarcerations, he was a model "inmate." He helped around our house, played with my son, and eventually painted the trim on our church, never having a single alcoholic drink. Again, with no responsibility or pressure, he had escaped his cycle.

During his stay, he received phone calls from family and "friends." Eventually, with the urging and insistence of his "friends," the local judge approved a short return visit.

During his return visit, the "friends" and local authorities convinced him to stay. He did and was again drunk within one week. His old environment, its influence, and his cycle had recaptured him.

Later, my mother finally and legally divorced him with a restraining order to vacate her property. He had to be fully responsible for himself for the first time in decades. He died in a prolonged drunkenness within the year.

Did he die because he couldn't break his cycle?

Did he die because he didn't have enough help?

Two Phone Calls

Phone call #1

I received a phone call that my aunt Rosie was in the hospital with cancer and would not live long. I responded that I would come immediately.

I quickly made arrangements for my local necessities and made plans to travel. I would leave, travel to Texas, pick up Curtis—my cousin who was just in on leave from the Air Force, Rosie's only adopted son—and drive immediately to the Lubbock Hospital to share Jesus Christ with my aunt and return home early the next morning.

Curtis was waiting when I arrived, and we immediately departed for the hospital. As I drove, I explained to Curtis what was about to take place—that upon arrival, once with my aunt, his mother, I would share Jesus Christ with my aunt to ascertain her acknowledgment.

As we drove on, I explained to Curtis exactly what that meant. I explained who Jesus is and his relevance to every human's eternity. I explained to Curtis that my mission was not to chitchat and rekindle old relationships. Assurance of my aunt's eternity was priority.

When we arrived at the hospital, I was still concluding these plans. We had not had time to share a long greeting or have our own chitchat.

Upon entering my aunt Rosie's room, she greeted us with her bright smile and cheery disposition. After her lavish gratitude for my trip, she explained that her surgery had been successful and the doctor had removed *all* her cancer (far from the actual truth).

I began sharing with Rosie my love and concern. We quickly moved past life conversation to eternal significance. To my great happiness, Rosie assured me of her salvation in Jesus Christ and explained in vivid detail her when, where, and how! How glorious of a testimony!

We had a celebratory prayer of praise, and Curtis and I soon left so my aunt could rest.

As I drove Curtis back to my uncle's home, I shared with Curtis my love for him and my aunt and the mission and purpose that Jesus had served.

As we pulled into his driveway very late that night and as Curtis opened the door to leave, I asked him if he had any questions about Jesus and about his relationship. He stepped out of the car, thanked me for coming, turned, and left.

As planned, I left very early the next morning to return home.

My aunt died a number of days later.

Phone call #2

Many years later, after the sale of my business, I, for a period of time, was working the midnight shift at a local Safeway. These hours made it possible for me to earn some income while I struggled to manage some legal problems and collections for my previous business sale that had been defaulted by the purchaser.

Being physically exhausted after each long overnight work shift, I would generally say "good morning/good night" to anyone around and immediately fall asleep in bed until late next evening prior to returning back to work.

This particular morning was going to be eternally different though.

Just before falling deep to sleep, Claudia awakened me with a phone call. I assumed it was a business call. No, she said it was an important call from my cousin Curtis in the Dallas, Texas, county jail!

I quickly sat up, took the phone, and tried to wake enough to organize my thought and speech.

Curtis immediately and joyously greeted me with the news that he was in the Dallas County Jail but had heard a visiting preacher tell the story and invitation of Jesus Christ and had accepted him as Savior and Lord because he remembered the night we had visited his mom in the hospital before her death.

Imagine
(John Lennon)

Imagine all the people
Livin' for today

…

Imagine there's no countries
It isn't hard to do
Nothing to kill or die for
And no religion, too
Imagine all the people
Livin' life in peace

…

Imagine no possessions
I wonder if you can
No need for greed or hunger
A brotherhood of man
Imagine all the people
Sharing all the world

…

You may say I'm a dreamer
But I'm not the only one
I hope someday you'll join us
And the world will be as one

So as you go about your new life, sharing the loving salvation offered by Jesus Christ, do not rush to conclusion or pressure.

God's love works in truly miraculous ways, methods, and timetables.

In many situations you will never know the eternal end result of your Christ-sharing love. Yet at times, God may share the results immediately or many years later.

For questions or comments, please contact Goddoesloveyou777@gmail.com.

About the Author

James was the youngest child captured in an extremely dysfunctional family. The child of parents and siblings of repeated *cycles* of failed marriages, relationships, and alcohol, drugs, and physical, mental and sexual abuse (https://jimiveymsm.wixsite.com/jamesivey).

James had no positive care or mentorship from any family, friend, school, or church. In his communities, he was neglected, invisible, and shunned. There was no help for "someone like him!"

In his own drunken, drugged attempt to finally advocate for his repeatedly beaten mother, late in one night on the verge of a final mental breakdown, he dragged his father into his backyard, beating him and tying him to a pole to kill and crucify.

He was startled, and his task was cut short by an audience shouting him down and *him* being blamed as the problem and reason of his miserable cycle.

Suicide seemed the only remedy. Alas, he could not even complete that!

Everyone at some point in their life struggles and lacks understanding and guidance. Your degree of suffering varies depending on your environment, quality of family, friends, and community, and it is always stalking you.

Read the following pages and behold the love and abundant life James finally was gifted and now shares with others. His loving wife of over fifty years, three successful sons, and nine wonderful grandchildren are his abundant life.

As a husband, father, grandfather, businessperson, entrepreneur, designer, educator, and author, James has now had college degrees, successful businesses, major national corporate positions, and professorships at numerous recognized colleges and universities.

He was shown how to break his cycle and create a new life!

Yes, everyone—even you—can break your cycle and create a new life!